COUPLES
CONVERSATIONS™
Vol 1.

Strengthen Your Foundation

Dr. Ari Sytner, LCSW, M.Ed, PhD

Looking For More Ways Improve your Relationship?

Check out all 5 volumes, as well as additional resources, videos and materials at:

www.couples-conversations.com

- Bonus relationship guides
- Free expert videos
- Self-paced lessons & courses
- Additional books
- Relationship quizzes
- Downloadable tools and printables resources

Couples Conversations™

© 2025 Ari Sytner, Couples Conversations™

All rights reserved. Published by Couples Conversations Press
New York • New Jersey
Ein Od Milvado

www.asytner.com

This book is intended for educational purposes only and is not for diagnosis, treatment, therapy, or any form of clinical mental-health intervention.

DEDICATION

To my best friend, Chana, who truly knows me, loves me, and inspires me every day of this crazy adventure we call life.

TABLE OF CONTENTS

INTRODUCTION

Why I Wrote This Book

When I was a freshly minted couples therapist, having completed my PhD and chasing my passion as a licensed clinical social worker, I hit the ground running. With the best training and the highest level of certification from the Gottman Institute, I was eager to help couples reduce conflict, improve communication, and rekindle their emotional and physical intimacy.

It has certainly been an incredible journey, and I feel deeply grateful to go to work every day doing what I love—helping couples strengthen their relationships and rediscover their connection.

Yet, over the past several years, I began noticing a troubling shift in the couples I was seeing. More were describing a kind of emotional distance I hadn't encountered as frequently before. I was noticing more disconnected, checked-out couples and less passionate, charged conflict.

Was it due to our increased screen time and dependence on technology? Was it a residual effect of pandemic lockdowns and prolonged isolation? I couldn't say for certain. But what I could see clearly was a growing pattern: couples describing a nightly routine where they lie in bed, each silently scrolling on their own devices before shutting off the lights and going to sleep.

No conversation. No connection. No intimacy.

Then, when couples finally wanted to chat, they would often report not knowing what to talk about.

When that cycle repeats, day after day, month after month, it gradually becomes the norm. Eventually, many couples find themselves struggling to re-engage and reconnect, wondering when the closeness faded and worrying if there is a path back to it.

Seeing this new reality compelled me to ask:

How can I help empower ordinary, intelligent couples to bridge that emotional divide and guide them back to meaningful conversation?

When I searched for tools to recommend, I found plenty of games and lighthearted books intended to spark dialogue. Many were fun and creative—but they weren't clinically grounded, rooted in research, or based on what I was hearing in real time from couples in therapy.

Therefore, I decided to create something that was both clinically informed, scientifically grounded, and highly practical.

As a researcher and professor who gets excited about data, I immersed myself in the science of successful relationships. I reviewed current research, integrated it with my years of clinical experience, and identified 15 foundational topics that happy, healthy couples tend to engage in over time.

These include the "big" topics, like money, sex, and parenting, but also the deeply personal ones that actually shape emotional safety and secure attachment in a healthy relationship.

As this book is the first in the series, it begins with the most essential layer: the foundation. It is in this very bedrock where the fate of the relationship is shaped.

What is it that makes a strong foundation?

Surprisingly, it is not about love or emotions, but about knowledge. It all begins with how well you know yourself, your partner, and your shared origin story. When a couple is armed with this knowledge it seeds the fertile ground for so much more to develop emotionally, as well as have the firm roots to help them unite and withstand any pressures or challenges that later come their way.

It is only with this foundation that a solid relationship can rest on a platform of mutual understanding, connection, respect and emotional safety.

Often couples who struggle with conflict or disconnection search far and wide for the answers of how to fix their relationship. They go on exotic vacations or buy luxurious gifts in the hopes of finding what is missing. Yet, in many cases, the answer is right at their feet. When aspects of their foundation are shaky and they lack an awareness of who they are, or an understanding of they are with, it will likely result in countless areas of struggles in the future. This book is designed to help you explore and discuss those missing pieces and firmly solidify that foundation.

The conversations in this volume will guide you back to the basics: asking, discussing, learning, listening and remembering why you chose each other. And as you move through this book and into future volumes — exploring conflict, parenting, intimacy, and more — you'll continue completing the puzzle of your unique partnership, one conversation at a time.

This foundational book invites couples to explore a range of conversations from childhood experiences to dating memories, and all of the things that make you who you are as individuals and as a couple.

As with every question in the Couples Conversations™ series, the questions in this book were created with intention and purpose, aiming to spark connection across multiple dimensions, such as emotional, intellectual, psychological, spiritual, and even existential.

It is my true hope that these conversations help you rediscover one another—not just as partners in life, but with the respect and understanding of dynamically evolving individuals worthy of acceptance, care, attention, and lasting love.

— Dr. Ari Sytner, PhD, LCSW, M.Ed

FOUNDATIONS:
Strengthening What You Cannot See

We are *"Fine"*

Several years ago, a couple sat across from me and explained that they were not in crisis. They were responsible parents. Their home was stable. They did not scream at each other. They were not considering separation. There had been no betrayal, no dramatic rupture. When I asked how they would describe their marriage, they both used the same word. *"Fine."*

As they continued speaking, something subtle began to surface. They could describe their children's schedules in detail and outline their financial plans with precision. They knew exactly how their week operated. What they struggled to articulate was how they felt about each other in the present moment. When I asked when they last had a conversation that was not about logistics, both of them froze. It had been a long time.

While they cared deeply about one another, they were no longer actively curious about each other. This is how drift often begins.

It does not arrive with drama. It unfolds gradually while life is being built and fatigue becomes normal. Under the best of circumstances, the relationship becomes efficient, predictable, and responsible. From the outside, everything appears intact. Internally, something less visible begins to fracture.

Many couples assume that if there is no explosive conflict, the relationship must be healthy. Yet decades of research in relationship science suggest something more nuanced. Long-term stability is shaped not only by the absence of crisis, but by the presence of emotional attunement and shared meaning. Couples who thrive over time maintain a living understanding of one another's inner world. They revisit, update, and constantly recalibrate to meet the ongoing changes and evolutions that life brings.

When understanding stalls, misinterpretations quietly increase. A minor comment feels sharper than it should. A small disappointment lingers longer than expected. Partners begin reacting not only to what is happening in the moment, but to what it represents to them, inside their own quiet and often lonely echo chamber.

Remembering Who You Were

Every couple carries an origin story. How you met; what initially drew you together; the uncertainty, excitement, and hope that marked your early days. Those stories are not just cute and sentimental memories. They form the narrative identity of your relationship.

Research examining marital resilience consistently shows that couples who can describe their beginnings with warmth and cohesion are more likely to withstand future stress. The story of "us" itself becomes stabilizing. It reinforces the sense that you are part of something shared and intentional. When couples remember how they once chose each other, it becomes easier to choose each other again during times of stress and tension.

However, when that shared narrative fades, conflict begins to feel personal and isolating. Disagreements become about winning or losing rather than protecting something shared that you both jointly created. Remembering your story will not erase problems, but it helps you shift perspective. It reminds you that you are both on the same team, even when you are struggling to understand each other in the moment.

Revisiting your story is not about romanticizing the past. It is about reinforcing identity. It is about asking who we were when we began, and what elements of that early connection still deserve attention now.

Many aspects of a relationship are like muscles that can be strengthened. When you fondly retell your origin story, you are strengthening your relationship muscle to help you again in the present. Just as you once scripted the story of who you are as a couple, you can rescript it again and again to shape yourselves into the couple you wish to become.

Choosing the Relationship You Want

The chapters that follow move intentionally through these layers. First, you will revisit your shared beginnings. Then, you will deepen your understanding of each other's inner world and update your working knowledge of one another and how you may have changed over time. Finally, you will clarify the partnership you are actively shaping and nurture the shared "we" aspect of your relationship.

These movements deliberately complement and reinforce one another. Remembering strengthens identity. Identity deepens understanding. Understanding makes collaboration possible. Collaboration sustains your story. These are the scientific ingredients needed for a healthy relationship foundation.

Strong relationships are rarely sustained by love alone. They are sustained by awareness, curiosity, and the willingness to examine what cannot be seen on the surface. They are strengthened when two people slow down long enough to really see each other and stay curious about how to know, understand, and really love each other.

As you move into these chapters, take your time. This is not a checklist to complete. It is an opportunity to realign, to update your understanding, and to choose the direction you want to move in together. Strengthening what cannot be seen may be the most important investment you make in the visible life you are building side by side. The goal here is not to be "fine" and hobble along year after year, but to be a truly strong and united team who are deeply committed to each other.

PUTTING DOWN THE PHONE,

Picking Up the Conversation

Let's be honest—when was the last time you and your partner had a conversation that wasn't about logistics, kids, bills, work, or what to watch on Netflix?

Remember a time when you first met, and you would talk for hours on end? Can you recall those late-night conversations where you lost track of time, discovering each other's worlds? Those were beautiful moments where "couples conversations" took you places with very little effort.

13

Yet, somewhere between mortgage payments, career demands, and the hypnotic glow of smartphones, those conversations can fade away. One day you look up and realize you're sharing a home but living in separate mental universes.

As a couples therapist, I see this dynamic day in and day out: couples sitting on my couch, genuinely caring about each other but no longer curious about each other. They can recite their partner's coffee order by heart but have no idea what stresses weigh on them at night, what victories they're secretly proud of, or what dreams they're hoping for in the coming years.

This isn't anyone's fault. Life gets busy, digital distractions multiply, and before you know it, years have gone by, and you're thinking, "I already know everything important about this person." However, the reality is that neither of you is the same as when you met years ago. As we advance through life, change is inevitable, leading to a distance that grows over time. In a sneaky way, this disconnection doesn't happen all at once—it creeps in slowly during times of blessing and stress and is often disguised as what others see as a successful couple, seemingly a well-oiled machine, able to juggle anything life throws at them.

When Conversation Fades, So Does Connection

The statistics are sobering. Dr. John Gottman, the world's leading researcher on relationships, found that the average couple speaks for only about 35 minutes per week, and much of that conversation revolves around errands, logistics, and other practical matters! That's roughly five minutes a day of actual communication—barely enough time to coordinate schedules, let alone connect on a meaningful level.

When couples stop talking, disconnection starts to creep in. Suddenly, you might find yourself surprised (and not in a good way) by your partner's reactions. Living parallel lives means that you're operating on outdated information about each other, and you may be completely unaware of what matters now to them more than ever. Small irritations that could be easily addressed build up into resentments because they are not shared nor compassionately heard. When disconnection settles in, life's daily victories go uncelebrated, emotions get bottled up, and loneliness takes over. As a result of this distance, physical intimacy tends to dwindle as emotional connection flickers. This is when couples start reporting that they feel like roommates. As this dynamic evolved over time, most can't pinpoint where the rift developed.

While many couples recognize this state of what I call "parallel living" and feel as though they are "fine," years of research on relationships have found that "fine" is a dangerous place to be. You might be handling the logistics of life together brilliantly but secretly experiencing a quiet loneliness that begins to grow. It is that void which becomes the seed for future problems to take root in the relationship.

But here's the good news: **disconnection isn't permanent**.

I often tell the couples I work with that the goal of couples therapy is not learning communication but building true connection. Whenever there is distance between two people, it feels as though there is a locked door between them, preventing them from reaching one another. Communication is simply the key to unlocking that door. With the right communication tools, couples can reawaken curiosity, stimulate interest in one another, rebuild connection and excitement, and fall in love all over again.

The Solution:
Couples Conversations™

The antidote to conversational drought isn't complicated. You don't need a relationship overhaul or dramatic gestures, but it does require intention. Once you have the desire to invest in building connection, the next thing you need is something to talk about. You need questions—good ones—and the willingness to listen to the answers as you explore each other's inner worlds with genuine interest and curiosity.

That's what this book provides: thoughtfully crafted questions that bypass the surface layers and invite you into territories worth exploring together. These aren't generic conversation starters. They're doorways that peer into deeper aspects of yourselves and your relationship—your memories, values, fears, hopes, and the unique culture you've created together.

Some questions will make you laugh. Some might make you tear up. Others will reveal things you never knew about the person with whom you share your life.

There are two goals that you will accomplish through these questions:

1. You will <u>experience the connection</u> that comes with the exploration of each other's hearts and minds.

2. By practicing these exchanges, you will <u>build the muscle of curiosity</u> that will make it intuitive and natural to maintain connection throughout your relationship.

When You're Ready for More

If you find these conversations meaningful and want to explore specific areas of your relationship more deeply, you'll find companion volumes to this book. Each contains hundreds of additional questions on topics like intimacy, communication, conflict, sex, parenting, money, dreams, and more.

Think of these companion books as specialized tools in your relationship toolkit—resources to support your ongoing journey of discovery together. They continue to offer new pathways of understanding and connection as your relationship evolves.

A Note About Professional Support

Talking should be simple and easy, right? Well, for many couples, frustrations arise along the way and they quickly get sucked into cycles of conflict. If you find that certain discussions consistently lead to conflict or disconnection despite your best efforts, it's not a sign of failure, but valuable information.

Professional support from a highly qualified couples therapist can provide a structured environment to safely learn and practice communication skills that better serve your relationship. A properly-trained couples therapist will not try to solve your problems, but help you develop the tools to solve your own issues and strengthen connection for years to come. I always tell couples that the goal of therapy is not communication but friendship. Good communication is simply the key you will need to access that friendship. Once a couple is fluent in effective communication, they can most likely put their heads and hearts together to work out most issues on their own.

If you notice recurring communication difficulties or escalations that result from these frustrations, consider reaching out for support. Just as you wouldn't hesitate to consult a doctor for your physical health, an attorney for legal help, feel free to reach out to a qualified couples therapist to help your relationship when challenges arise. While these books are going to open up worlds of conversations, they are not intended to replace clinical support and therapy for those who suffer from mental-health challenges and require professional support.

One Final Thought

In my years of working with couples, I've noticed something interesting: the happiest pairs aren't those with the fewest problems or the most impressive achievements. They're the ones who maintain genuine curiosity about each other and never stop asking questions to learn more about the person they love.

This book is an invitation to reclaim that curiosity. To remember that your partner isn't a known quantity but a mystery you get to keep unpacking and exploring. To recognize that the most valuable gift you can give each other isn't expensive jewelry or grand gestures, but the simple, profound act of paying attention and showing you care.

The pages ahead hold not just questions, but possibilities—for deeper understanding, renewed appreciation, and the kind of connection that makes all the logistics and challenges of shared life worthwhile. So pour that coffee (or wine), put the phones away, look each other in the eyes, take a slow, deep breath, and rediscover the person you love.

HOW TO USE THIS BOOK
(The Practical Stuff)

Below are 15 principles to help you get the most from these conversations. Think of them as guideposts for emotional connection, not rigid rules, but supportive habits that can help you get the most out of this book and your relationship.

Remember: this isn't a "read cover-to-cover" kind of book. It's a conversation tool to be dipped into, explored, and revisited over time. Some days you may feel drawn to deeper, more reflective topics. Other days, something light or playful might be just right. There's no set path here. Follow your energy and curiosity, not a rigid sequence.

1. SCHEDULE IT

Yes, scheduling a conversation might sound unromantic, like penciling in passion. But here's the truth: if it's not planned, it probably won't happen. Life is full of interruptions and responsibilities, and good intentions often get swallowed by the day-to-day.

Setting a regular time for connection, maybe Sunday mornings over coffee or Thursday nights after the kids go to bed, creates consistency. It turns talking into a meaningful ritual that you look forward to, not just something you squeeze in when everything else is done. Block out anywhere from 10 to 30 minutes where your only focus is each other. That small investment pays huge dividends in deepening emotional closeness.

2. CREATE PHONE-FREE ZONES

As much as we love our devices, they are serious distractions. Even a buzzing notification or glance at the screen can pull a couple out of a meaningful moment. The best thing to do is either power off your phones for a few minutes or put them in another room. The message in doing so is: "You matter more to me than anything that might show up on this screen."

It may feel uncomfortable at first, but the quiet it creates is fertile ground for real connection. You're not just removing distractions; you're reclaiming each other's full attention.

3. START SMALL

These questions are intended for quality over quantity. Don't overload your time with too many questions. You are not on a game show trying to shout out the "right answers" under a ticking clock.

Instead, start with one or two well-chosen questions and go deep. Let the conversation unfold naturally. One powerful exchange is worth far more than a dozen rushed answers. You're not here to check boxes; rather, you're here to slow down, connect, and discover each other together.

4. SET A POSITIVE TONE

Your environment sets the emotional stage. While we can't always have the perfect environment, there are always things we can do to enhance the mood. This may include turning on soft music in the background, sharing a cup of tea or a glass of wine, enjoying your favorite snacks, or simply sitting together in a cozy, quiet spot. The goal is to signal to your nervous system: this is safe, warm, and inviting.

When both people feel relaxed, curiosity and vulnerability flow more easily. You're not performing or fixing anything; you're simply sharing a moment of closeness.

5. APPROACH IT LIKE A DATE

Remember the thrill of those early conversations? You likely were not multitasking or half-listening, but were fully present, eager to know more. When you wipe the slate clean and assume that you don't really know the other person, it lends itself to sparking real curiosity, as when you first dated. That same energy is still available to you now. Your partner may be familiar, but they're not fully known. People change. Layers emerge. Interests shift. This is your chance to be reintroduced to each other, again and again. Treat these moments as discovery, not obligation.

6. TAKE YOUR TIME WITH EACH QUESTION

Think of the questions as doorways into meaningful territory, not items to quickly "get through." When you open up a question, stay in it; swim in those waters together and let one question lead to memories, stories, emotions, laughter, or even gentle silence. One thoughtful conversation that stays with you for days is more powerful than rushing through a list.

7. USE YOUR BODY TO COMMUNICATE

Nonverbal signals matter just as much as words. Turn toward each other. Make eye contact. Nod. Smile. Hold hands if that feels right. Use your whole body to say, "I'm here with you."

These small gestures foster trust and emotional safety. They show your partner they're not just being heard; they're being felt.

8. PRACTICE POSITIVE CURIOSITY

Curiosity is the lifeblood of long-term connection. Without it, we assume we already know our partner, when in reality, people change, and we risk missing those updates. Curiosity is the tool that allows us to keep falling in love again and again. It says, "I care enough to learn more." Instead of assuming you know your partner's thoughts or story, choose to explore them again with fresh eyes. Listen for the parts you've never heard before or the nuances that were never fully unpacked.

Remember that if curiosity opens the door, judgment slams it shut. When you are the one asking a question, your job is to really listen to your partner. Do your best to remove all judgment or preconceived ideas, even if you have a completely different opinion. In a curious state of mind, you can wonder and learn about the other's views and get to know how they see the world—rather than try to share why you disagree.

A great technique for staying in that curious role is to ask follow-up questions. As you read the questions in this book, you will notice that most have a follow-up aimed at helping you dig deeper. Be sure to add your own as the conversations unfold.

For example:

- "What was that like for you?"

- "Tell me more about that."

- "What made that moment matter so much to you?"

- "How could I better support you?"

Avoid questions that interrogate or criticize (especially when your partner is being vulnerable):

- "Are you sure that's how it happened?"

- "Why do you make everything so dramatic?"

- "Well, that's not true. Didn't you say the opposite last time?"

The key to good listening is not to contradict or argue with your partner's perspective, but to remain open to seeing the world through their eyes. These curious conversations are not about right or wrong, or setting the record straight, rather how to gain a deeper understanding of the other, especially when you have a different view.

9. LISTEN MORE THAN YOU SPEAK

One of the greatest gifts you can give your partner is undivided, non-defensive attention. Let them share without interruption. Listen not to reply, but to understand.

Use simple signals: nods, soft "mmhmm" sounds, leaning in slightly. Think of it like enjoying a slow, delicious meal to be savored, not swallowed.

10. AFFIRM THEIR SHARING

Vulnerability can be scary, even in committed relationships. When your partner opens up, create safety by showing them you are holding what they are saying with care. Try to affirm it by saying something like:

- "Thank you for telling me that."

- "That was brave to share."

- "I really appreciate your honesty."

- "I loved learning about that side of you."

- "It felt really good to laugh together like that."

This builds emotional safety. When someone knows they'll be met with respect and gratitude, not correction or criticism, they're more likely to open up again.

11. TAKE A BREATHER IF NEEDED

Not every conversation will feel light and easy. Some questions may surface deeper emotions or even disagreements. That's okay. If the tension rises, take a slow breath and pause.

Say something like, "Let's come back to this when we're both feeling more centered." Then flip to a lighter prompt or take a short walk. Connection grows in safety, not pressure.

12. FOLLOW THE TANGENTS

These questions are meant to be starting points, not scripts. If one response leads you into a totally different memory, story, or insight, just follow it. Resist the urge to pull your partner back to the question at hand, and try to go with the flow wherever it takes you.

Sometimes the richest conversations grow from those unplanned detours. Trust the process. The goal is not to "finish the page," but to rediscover each other along the way.

13. REFLECTING ON EACH CHAPTER

At the end of each chapter, you'll find a set of reflection questions designed to help you process and personalize your conversations. These prompts aren't quizzes or tests, they're invitations. Use them as a way to slow down, notice what stood out, and uncover insights that may not have surfaced in the moment. Simply by revisiting and processing what was learned or discovered can help deepen the feeling of connectedness.

You can answer these questions together in dialogue, take turns responding, or even journal your answers separately and share them later. However you choose to engage, this space is meant to deepen your learning and solidify the growth that's unfolding in your relationship, one conversation at a time.

14. SKIP AROUND THE BOOK

You will notice checkboxes next to each question. These are there to invite you to jump around to the questions that speak to you and not to feel the pressure of going in order. Just check off the questions you've discussed as you go and enjoy the journey of wherever the questions take you. (For a real challenge, feel free to revisit checked questions later and see if new conversation emerge).

15. HAVE FUN!

Take a breath and remember to laugh and have fun. This experience is the feeling of going deeper into one another's inner world, building connection and strengthening your shared love. That should be something worth enjoying!

QUICK SUMMARY FOR
MEANINGFUL CONVERSATIONS

1. **Schedule it**: Set intentional time for meaningful connection.

2. **Go phone-free**: Eliminate distractions; give undivided attention.

3. **Start small:** Focus on quality over quantity of questions.

4. **Set the tone**: Environment should feel calm, safe, and inviting.

5. **Treat it like a date**: Be present and curious.

6. **Go deep, not fast**: Stay with emotionally significant moments instead of moving on too quickly.

7. **Use your body:** Eye contact, body language, and gentle touch.

8. **Practice curiosity**: Ask clarifying questions before reacting or forming conclusions.

9. **Listen to understand**: Resist the urge to defend or solve issues.

10. **Affirm vulnerability**: Show appreciation to openness.

11. **Pause when needed**: Slow or pause conversations if needed.

12. **Follow the tangents**: Just go with any organic detours.

13. **Reflect together**: Process what you learned after each chapter.

14. **Skip around**: Follow what interests you.

15. **Keep it Fun:** Remember that connection should feel energizing, not like an obligation.

CHAPTER 1

Building Our Story

*"In true love, you attain freedom.
You become one, not by losing yourself,
but by finding yourself in the other."*

— THICH NHAT HANH

Building Our Story

Take a moment to appreciate that there are more than seven billion people on the planet. The fact that the two of you found each other is nothing short of extraordinary. Yet, in some ways, finding each other is the easy part; strengthening those bonds and remaining forever connected through life's ups and downs is a lifelong task.

According to the research of Dr. John Gottman, world-renowned relationship expert, every couple has an origin story: the unique way you met, fell in love, and chose to build a life together. Research shows these narratives aren't just sentimental; they're powerful forces that shape the foundation and resilience of your future relationship.

In fact, couples who savor their origin story and revel in the details of how their relationship developed tend to show greater resilience during challenging times. These partners can readily access specific, positive memories from their shared history, creating a reservoir of positivity to tap into during difficult times. Holding positive memories of the relationship becomes an emotional buffer, allowing couples to navigate conflict with a deeper sense of perspective.

This kind of reminiscing isn't just nostalgic; it's neurologically powerful. When you recall positive relationship memories together, your brain releases oxytocin, the bonding hormone that deepens emotional closeness. In effect, when you revel in your story, you're rewiring your brain to associate your relationship with safety, joy, and connection.

What makes your shared story especially meaningful is how it blends two unique perspectives. You might remember the vibrant red sweater your partner wore on your first date, while they recall exactly what you ordered for dinner. One of you may have felt sure about the relationship from the start, while the other experienced a gradual awakening to deeper feelings. These complementary memories don't cancel each other out. Instead, they weave together to form a richer, more textured narrative than either of you could create alone.

Even long-term couples often uncover unexplored details of their own story. You may never have known what your partner told their best friend after meeting you, or what doubts they had to overcome before committing fully.

The questions and prompts below are designed to create space for those revelations—deepening your understanding not just of what happened—but of what it meant to each of you along the way.

As you explore these questions, resist the urge to correct your partner's version of events. The emotional truth of how a moment felt to your partner matters more than perfect factual alignment. By approaching these conversations with openness and curiosity, you'll likely discover new layers to a story you thought you already knew.

By consciously cultivating and celebrating your relationship's origin story, you're not just honoring your past; you're strengthening your present and laying the foundation for all the chapters still to come. The narrative you share becomes both anchor and compass: a reminder of where you've been and a guide for where you're going together.

THE VERY BEGINNING

1

What do you remember about the very first time you saw me? Can you recall how I looked, what I wore, or any specific details that caught your attention?

2

When you tell people the story of how we met, what details do you always include? What parts still make you smile every time?

3

What was running through your mind during our first real conversation? Was there a moment when something just clicked?

4

Remember that text or call you made to a friend or relative after our first date? What did you say about me that surprised even you?

5

☐ What little thing did I do early on that made you think, "This might be different from other relationships"? When did you first feel that spark of possibility?

6

☐ What are some highlights from our dating days that still stand out in your mind? Which dates or moments feel most vivid?

7

☐ What are some hilarious or awkward moments from our early dates that we can laugh about now? How did we handle those moments at the time?

8

☐ Where did we go on our third date, and why was that one particularly memorable? What happened that moved us forward?

9

☐ What was our first big milestone as a new couple? How did we celebrate or mark that moment?

10

☐ When did we first travel together, even if just for a weekend? What did that trip reveal about us?

FALLING IN LOVE

11

☐ What do you remember about how it felt when you were falling in love with me?

12

☐ What do you remember about the first time we said "I love you" to each other? Who said it first and how did it happen?

13

☐ When was the moment you realized this relationship was the real thing? What shifted from casual to serious for you?

14

☐ When our relationship first got serious, what qualities about me made you excited to be with me forever?

15

☐ What conversation early on made you realize we could talk about anything? When did communication feel effortless?

16

☐ When did you first use the word boyfriend, girlfriend, or partner to describe me? What did it feel like and what did it mean to you?

MEETING EACH OTHER'S WORLDS

17

What was going through your mind when you first introduced me to your parents? How did that meeting unfold?

18

Which friend of yours was the first to meet me, and what was their initial reaction? Did they predict we'd last?

19

What was it like bringing me to your hometown or showing me where you grew up? What stories did you share?

20

When did we first attend a wedding or major event together as a couple? How did that feel different from going solo?

21

What family tradition of yours did I experience first? How did I handle being the newcomer?

22

What hobby or interest did we discover together? What became an early shared passion?

23

Were there any quirks from your inner world that you were hesitant to share with me, or were worried might scare me away?

OUR "FIRSTS"

24

When was the first time we said "we" about future plans? What were we planning together?

25

☐ What was our first holiday together like? How did we decide whose family to visit or what traditions to follow?

26

☐ Do you remember our first fight or serious disagreement? How did we resolve it, and what did we learn?

27

☐ What was the first gift you ever gave me with love in your heart? Why did you choose it?

28

☐ When did separate friend groups begin merging into shared friendships? Who became "our" friends first?

29

☐ What was the first piece of furniture we bought together and what do you remember about that experience?

30

☐ When did we establish our first "couple routine"? What pattern or ritual became uniquely ours?

31

☐ When did we first combine finances in any way— splitting rent, sharing groceries, or planning a budget? What did that feel like for you?

32

☐ What was the first major decision we made together? How did we approach that choice, and how would we approach it differently today?

33

When did you first notice we were developing our own language—inside jokes, references, or shorthand? Are there any that still stand out?

34

When it comes to marking our first anniversaries, which moments do you celebrate: our first date, first kiss, engagement, marriage, and why?

35

When did we first appear together in a family photo or holiday card? How official did that feel?

36

When was the first time one of us went through an illness or health scare? How did that level of vulnerability feel at the time? How did we handle it?

37

Are there any other earlier "firsts" or anniversaries that we have overlooked but can now start to celebrate? How can we make those events feel more special?

MEMORABLE MOMENTS

38

What's our "origin story" that we tell differently to different people? How do we edit our tale for various audiences?

39

When people ask how we met, what's one proud detail you never leave out? What makes that element essential to our story?

40

☐ Is there a specific part of our story that we deliberately leave out when telling people how our relationship began?

41

☐ Which photo from our early days best captures how we were then? What story does that image tell?

42

☐ What restaurant became "our place" early on? Why did we keep returning there?

43

☐ What movie or TV show did we binge together that became part of our couple culture? Were there any themes or lines that became a part of us?

44

Which concert, play, or event did we attend that felt like a defining date? What made it special?

GROWING TOGETHER

45

What difficult challenge did we face early in our relationship that proved we could handle hardships together? Do you remember how it felt at the time compared to how it feels in hindsight?

46

What early compromise showed you we could balance both our needs? How did we find middle ground?

47

When did planning together stop feeling like negotiation and start feeling like we were collaborating on the same team? Can you recall a story of this?

48

What behavior or habit of mine did you adopt without realizing it? When did you notice this influence?

49

How long were we together before you felt comfortable being completely yourself? Can you share an example? What changed?

50

What achievement did one of us reach that the other joined in celebration as if it were their own? When did individual success turn into a shared one?

TAKING NEXT STEPS

51

What made you certain you wanted to take the next big step with me? Was there a specific moment or gradual realization?

52

When did conversations shift from "if" to "when" regarding our future? What plans became certainties?

53

What was the first wedding we attended where we caught ourselves imagining our own? Did it make you feel more excited or nervous about our own future?

54

Do you remember when we started keeping things at each other's places? Whose toothbrush moved in first, and what did that say about our relationship?

55

What moment or conversation led to the decision that we wanted to spend our lives together? What do you recall about how that felt?

56

How did it feel for you when we moved in together? What stands out about that big step?

TRANSITIONAL MOMENTS

57

When did "hanging out" become "dating" in your mind? What shifted your perception?

58

How did we navigate the transition from casual to committed? What conversations marked that change?

59

When did you first imagine a future with me? What daydream included us together long-term?

60

☐ What external event or circumstance pushed us closer together? How did outside forces affect our bond?

61

☐ Do you remember a time at the start of our relationship when we had to prioritize each other over our parents or siblings? What was that like?

LOOKING BACK NOW

62

☐ Which year of our relationship brought the most growth? What major changes came during those twelve months?

63

☐ Was there a pattern that formed in our early days which still defines how we interact today? Which dynamics remained constant?

64

☐ What prediction did someone make about us that proved true? Whose insight was spot-on?

65

☐ If you could relive the most wonderful phase of our relationship, which would it be and why?

66

☐ Can you tell me about an early part of our story that you wish you could redo? What would be different?

67

☐ What joyful story from our beginning do you hope we never forget? Which memory deserves preserving?

68

How has your perspective on our early days changed with time? What do you understand now that you didn't then?

69

What worry or fear from our early days makes you smile now because it turned out to be so unnecessary? When did that anxiety transform into confidence?

70

If you had a time machine, what do you wish you could tell your younger self prior to our first date? How might that have changed anything about our story?

BUILDING BLOCKS

71

What was one small decision that we made early on that turned out to have bigger implications than we expected?

72

☐ When did we establish boundaries with work, friends, or family that protected our relationship? How did we claim our space?

73

☐ What do you remember about our early conversations about money? How did we handle discussions about finances?

74

☐ What boundary should we have established early on? How might that have helped strengthen our relationship?

75

☐ When did we first create our own holiday traditions? How did we blend or break from family patterns? What was it like for you to do?

Uniquely Us

76

☐ What would someone need to know to truly understand our relationship's beginning? What context matters most?

77

☐ How did timing play a role in our story? Why was meeting when we did significant?

78

☐ What inside joke from our first year still makes us laugh? How did that shared humor develop?

79

☐ When did we develop our conflict resolution style? What early disagreement taught us how to argue well?

80

☐ What made you think, "This person gets me" in a way others hadn't? When did understanding feel effortless?

81

☐ What mistakes from our early days actually helped shape who we've become? How did those stumbles secretly strengthen us?

82

☐ When did we first host others as a couple? How did entertaining together feel? Would you do anything differently today?

83

☐ What's a weird food combination or drink that we enjoy that others might think is crazy? If we don't have one, can we create one?

SNAPSHOTS IN TIME

84

What song was playing during a pivotal moment in our early relationship? What do you feel today when that same song comes on?

85

What season did we meet in, and how did that affect our early dates? How does the weather today trigger memories of our dating?

86

What news event or cultural moment was happening when we first got together? What backdrop surrounded our beginning?

87

Which friend's relationship did we admire early on? What couple modeled something we wanted?

88

What book, movie, or shared cultural reference became significant to us? How did media become memory?

PRIVATE MOMENTS

89

When did we first share something deeply personal? What vulnerable story created new intimacy?

90

What was it like for you the first time we touched? What about our first kiss?

91

What was an early moment when you wished I understood you better? How would you communicate those feelings differently now?

92

When did you first see me truly upset or struggling? How did vulnerability change our dynamic?

93

What late-night conversation went deeper than expected? Which talk lasted until dawn?

94

When did you first imagine introducing me to someone important who wasn't around anymore? What would you have wanted them to know?

95

Do you remember a time falling asleep while talking with each other, either in person or over the phone? How does it make you feel to think about?

96

When we were dating, can you remember that feeling of being excited to see each other again? What memories can you share about those moments?

OUR CONTINUING STORY

97

If you wrote a relationship book based on our story, what lessons would you want young couples to learn from our wins and struggles?

98

Who should we forever be grateful to for helping us find each other? How can we continue to express that gratitude?

99

☐ What theme runs through our entire relationship from day one? What thread connects all chapters?

100

☐ What is an important aspect of our story that we tend to easily forget or take for granted? What could we do to keep it more at the forefront of our minds?

CHAPTER 1:
AFTER THE CONVERSATION

As you complete this chapter, take a moment to pause and reflect. You've just revisited one of the most meaningful stories you share: the origin of your relationship. These conversations weren't just about remembering what happened, but about reconnecting with how it felt and why it mattered.

In sharing the details of how you met, what drew you to one another, and how your story unfolded, you've honored something sacred: your beginnings. Whether your journey started with instant chemistry or a slow-burning friendship, you've each brought your own perspective, memories, and emotions to the experience.

Revisiting your story isn't only about nostalgia, it's about strengthening the threads that still tie you together. Research shows that couples who actively cherish their origin story tend to show more resilience in difficult times. Why? Because when we remember where we started and what we overcame, we're reminded of what makes our bond worth protecting.

This kind of storytelling can also be powerfully grounding. It gives you a shared narrative to return to, not just as a memory, but as a compass. Thus, as you evolve together as a couple, the story can anchor you in where you begin, and evolve with you. It's not just a snapshot in time; it's a living part of your relationship identity.

Additionally, relationships are fueled by authentic moments of sharing vulnerability. When couples reflect back and share the private thoughts, feelings, and memories of when they first fell in love with each other, that experience itself creates deep connection.

Moments of laughter, uncertainty, excitement, and vulnerability are all threads in your shared tapestry. By revisiting them with curiosity and care, you've reinforced that your foundation really matters, and it is worth continuing to nurture through each next chapter of life.

What have we learned?

As you reflect on the conversations and responses from this chapter, ask yourselves the questions below. Take a few moments to discuss your answers and journal your response.

1. What aspects of our origin story stood out the most during this conversation, and what can we learn from it now?

    _____

    _____

    _____

2. What new discoveries, memories, or perspectives did we uncover from our early days together?

    _____

    _____

    _____

3. What do our individual versions of our story reveal about how we each experience love and connection? How can we use that to strengthen our bond in the future?

    _____

    _____

    _____

4. When difficult moments arise in our future, what are some aspects of our origin story that we can remind ourselves to help get us through it?

_____

_____

_____

5. What are some values, emotions, or themes that were present in our early story that we still want to develop and nurture today?

_____

_____

_____

6. What parts of our journey should we be most proud of, and why?

_____

_____

_____

7. As a result of these conversations, what is something you recalled about each other from your early days that made you smile or sparked feelings of love, and why?

_____

_____

_____

8. What are some romantic elements to our origin story that we may want to rekindle?

_____

_____

_____

9. What are some ways our relationship will be stronger as a result of the conversations we've discussed in this chapter?

_____

_____

_____

CHAPTER **2**

Getting to Know Each Other Deeply

"The greatest happiness of life is the conviction that we are loved; loved for ourselves, or rather, loved in spite of ourselves."

— *VICTOR HUGO*

Getting to Know Each Other Deeply

Think about the last time someone truly understood you. What was it like when someone anticipated exactly what you needed or responded gently after you had a rough day? That feeling of being deeply known creates a kind of emotional safety that nourishes a relationship at its roots.

Dr. John Gottman's research identified "Love Maps" as the foundation of strong, lasting relationships. These mental maps represent how well partners understand each other's inner world: their histories, values, triggers, goals, fears, and dreams. Couples with well-developed Love Maps tend to know each other deeply and can navigate challenges more successfully. This is because they deeply understand the emotional meaning behind each other's reactions. For example, when one partner comes home stressed, the other doesn't just see irritability; rather, they compassionately recognize the deeper pressures at play and respond with care instead of frustration or defensiveness.

It all starts with how well you know each other. The stronger your knowledge, the stronger your relationship can be. But here's the challenge: your partner cannot fully know you unless you know yourself. This is where an intimate relationship can hold up a mirror to allow you to take a deeper look within yourself and discover more about who you are.

Many people go through life on autopilot, rarely pausing to ask why certain situations hurt so deeply. They might recognize their emotional reactions but overlook the layers beneath, such as childhood experiences, parental dynamics, or past traumas that quietly shaped their attachment styles. These early moments often plant beliefs and patterns that guide us long after we've forgotten their origins.

By examining and sharing your patterns, beliefs, wounds, and hopes, you gain insight into where you come from and what drives you. This chapter is designed to offer space for that kind of gentle, honest self-exploration. It invites each of you to reflect on parts of yourselves that may not surface in daily conversation and explore formative memories, insecurities, values, and private needs, hopes, and dreams that shape who you are today.

When you share these inner dimensions with your partner, you create conditions that truly allow you both to be seen, accepted, and affirmed in your most vulnerable places. This kind of deep recognition fulfills one of our most fundamental needs: to be known and loved not just for what we do, but for who we truly are.

Some of what you uncover in these conversations may surprise you both, but that is a positive outcome. Since the nature of humans is that we are ever-evolving and always growing, there will likely be new aspects to discover about one another, even after you think you've heard it all.

Take your time with these questions and be gentle where needed. Some may spark immediate insight. Others might need to simmer for a while. Unlike a contestant on a trivia game show, the objective is not to hit the buzzer and shout out the right answer. It is to be thoughtful and curious with yourself and your partner. When both of you remain open to discovering more about one another, your relationship becomes a living space for growth, intimacy, and lasting connection.

FAMILY FOUNDATIONS

101

☐ What did marriage look like as a child watching your parents? Did you witness passionate kisses, heated arguments, a business partnership, or something else altogether?

102

☐ Tell me about your mother. What early memory of her stands out? How would you describe her presence in your childhood?

103

☐ Tell me about your father during your early years. How did his personality and involvement shape your development?

104

☐ How did your parents handle conflict? What did this teach you about handling disagreements?

105

Were your feelings as a child honored and validated, or were they more often dismissed? How did this impact you?

106

Was your family emotionally expressive or more reserved? How did you know if you were loved?

107

How were you disciplined as a child for acting out? How has that impacted you?

108

What role did your grandparents play in your upbringing? Were they the fun escape, wise counselors, strict traditionalists, or distant figures you barely knew?

109

Which aunt, uncle, or extended family member left the biggest impression on you? What made them stand out in your constellation of relatives?

CHILDHOOD ENVIRONMENT

110

Paint me a picture of the house you grew up in. What sounds, smells, and textures made it home? Can you walk me through a typical morning there?

111

Do you associate your childhood with feeling safe, anxious, supported, or alone? How does that foundation spill over into our relationship?

112

What was the emotional temperature of your household? Was it chaotic and loud, peaceful and predictable, tense and careful, or warm and welcoming?

113

Who was the most colorful character in your extended family? What outrageous stories about them still get repeated at gatherings?

114

What was dinnertime like at your house? Was it a sacred family gathering, grab-and-go chaos, or something you dreaded? What conversations happened around food?

115

What rituals or traditions from your childhood home still influence how you create comfort in your own space? Which ones did you consciously leave behind?

EARLY INFLUENCES

116

What TV show or movie from your youth shaped your idea of how relationships should work? How has that ideal evolved with reality?

117

What game or activities did you lose yourself in as a kid? What drew you to that particular escape?

118

Was there a teacher who saw something in you that you didn't see in yourself? What did they recognize, and how did their belief change your trajectory?

119

What playground dynamics taught you your first lessons about friendship, betrayal, or loyalty? Which recess dramas still influence how you navigate relationships?

GROWING UP MOMENTS

120

Tell me about your most epic childhood adventure—
planned or accidental. What did that escapade reveal
about your natural instincts?

121

What was your first taste of independence? Was it
walking to school alone, your first sleepover, or
something that just felt very grown-up at the time?
How do you feel about it in hindsight?

122

When did you first realize your family was different
from others? Was it a shocking revelation or gradual
awareness? How did this shape your own path?

123

What childhood fear seemed insurmountable at the
time but makes you smile now? What helped you
overcome it, or does it still lurk in some form?

124

□ Did you ever get in trouble or suspended from school? What happened? How did this affect you?

125

□ Was there a responsibility that was given to you when you were probably too young? How did this shape you?

126

□ When did you first realize that your parents were human and made mistakes along the way? What was that realization like for you?

127

□ Do you remember the first time you drank alcohol? Did you end up drinking too much? Can you tell me that story?

128

Who was your first romantic crush? Were you able to tell anybody? Did you ever try to act on it?

YOUR INNER WORLD

129

As a child, where did you go to feel completely safe and yourself? Was it a physical hideout, an imaginary world, or a state of mind?

130

What emotion did you struggle most to express growing up? How would it have been received in your home?

131

How did you self-soothe as a kid when things got tough? Are there any stories or examples you can share?

132

How did adversity shape parts of your personality growing up? Who were you able to turn to?

133

What part of yourself did you learn to hide in order to fit in or stay safe? When did you first feel free to let that authentic piece show?

134

Are there any experiences of pain, trauma, or abuse that you carry deep inside? Can you share them with me? How can I best honor those wounds and be sensitive toward them?

TASTES & PREFERENCES

135

What's your earliest food memory that still affects your preferences today? Is there a dish that instantly transports you back to childhood?

136

What weird food combination did you invent as a kid that you secretly (or not so secretly) still enjoy? What would others think if they knew?

137

Which childhood flavor or scent has strong memories associated? For instance, the smell of a certain foods being cooked or fresh-cut grass; where does this scent take you?

138

What colors are you naturally drawn to in your clothing, home, or surroundings? Is there a particular shade that feels distinctly "you," and why?

139

What comfort food instantly makes a bad day better, and is there a story behind why this dish has such power over your mood?

140

What's the most memorable meal you've ever had? Who was there? What did you eat? What made it so special?

141

Which food from your cultural heritage connects you most strongly to your roots? Is there a family recipe that's been passed down that you treasure?

142

If you could eat any dessert every day of the week, what would it be and why? Can you tell me about the very first time you tasted it?

143

What simple pleasure consistently brings you joy no matter how many times you experience it? When did you first discover this reliable source of happiness?

144

☐ How do you take your coffee? Does your order change based on any circumstances?

145

☐ If you could order anything from an open bar, what is your favorite beverage and why? When did you first taste it?

146

☐ What is your favorite flavor of ice cream? How would you prefer it: cup, cone, sprinkles, toppings, hot fudge?

EMERGING IDENTITY

147

☐ What moment in your teens felt like a clear "before and after" in your life story? How did that experience shape your path?

148

☐ Growing up, were friendships easy for you? Did you just fit in, or was it a challenge? Can you share any specific memories?

149

☐ Who was your first real friend—the one who showed you what genuine connection could be? What happened to that friendship?

150

☐ What subject in school gave you the feeling of confidence? What subject made you feel like you were destined to fail?

151

☐ When did you first feel like you truly belonged somewhere? Was it a place, a group, or a moment when you thought, "These are my people"?

152

What is a fun fact that you are proud to share with people? When did you first discover this about yourself?

153

What was your first favorite song or album that felt like "your music" rather than your parents' vibe? How did it speak to your emerging identity?

CURIOSITIES & FASCINATIONS

154

What rabbit hole topic can you spend hours researching? What does it feel like to lose yourself in it?

155

If you could master any skill overnight, what would revolutionize your life the most? What doors would that ability open?

156

What type of landscape makes your soul feel most at home? Are you a mountain person dreaming of peaks, or does the ocean's rhythm match your heartbeat? When did you first learn this about yourself?

157

Which historical era do you romanticize? If you could travel back in time, when and where would you visit, and why?

158

What future innovation do you most hope to see in your lifetime? What problem would you love to see solved?

DAILY RHYTHMS

159

What tiny ritual starts your day right? Is it that first coffee sip, stretching like a cat, or scrolling through overnight messages?

160

What constitutes a perfect day for you? Walk me through the simple pleasures that add up to contentment.

161

What sensory combinations instantly relax you? Is it dim lights, soft music, weighted blankets, white noise, soothing scents, physical touch, or something uniquely soothing?

162

Tell me about your happy place. Where do you go to reset when life feels overwhelming? Is it a physical place, mental exercise, or specific activity that brings you back to center?

163

What ordinary object or simple pleasure brings you disproportionate joy, and why?

SOCIAL MAPPING

164

☐ Does being social with others recharge your batteries or deplete you? How would you like me to be supportive of this dynamic?

165

☐ What quality in others makes you curious to want to get to know them better? What things turn you away?

166

☐ How has your definition of friendship evolved over time? What life experiences have shaped your definition of a true friend?

167

☐ In what setting do you feel most yourself? Is it intimate dinners, large celebrations, outdoor adventures, cozy home gatherings, or being in solitude? Why?

168

How do compliments land with you? When did you develop this response pattern? How can I best ensure that my compliments to you always land?

169

Who makes you laugh harder than anyone else in your life? What is it about their humor that connects so perfectly with yours?

PLAY & RECREATION

170

If you had a whole day with nothing to do, what would you naturally gravitate toward? What does your inner compass point to when obligation-free, and why?

171

What childhood game or activity do you still enjoy, such as building sandcastles or snowmen, swinging on swings, or coloring in coloring books? What does it feel like to act childlike?

172

What sport or physical activity reveals your true competitive nature (or lack thereof)? How do you handle winning and losing?

173

What's your relationship with nature? Is there a history to this feeling you can share with me?

174

Is there an outdoor activity that you truly live for, such as hiking, biking, skiing, kayaking, or something else? What is the story behind this activity?

Comfort & Care

175

How do you like to be taken care of when you're sick? Are you a "leave me alone to suffer" person, or do you prefer constant attention and comfort? How would you like me to show you I am here to support you?

176

Are there any indulgences that you truly value as forms of self-care? What are some things that restore you that you'd like me to be supportive of?

177

How does your energy shift with the seasons? Do you hibernate in winter, come alive in spring, or wilt in summer heat? What does it feel like to be you during those times?

Collections & Treasures

178

What do you collect, either intentionally or by accident? Books, memories, ticket stubs, or houseplants? What do these items mean to you?

179

What physical object in your daily life sparks joy every time you use it? What makes it special beyond its function?

180

What book or movie do you return to like an old friend—where you can quote lines by heart? When you dive into it, where does it take you?

181

What item in your wardrobe tells a story? Is there a concert tee, inherited watch, or lucky socks with meaning beyond their appearance?

182

If you could only save three possessions from a disaster, what would make the cut? What makes these items irreplaceable?

183

What family heirloom connects you to your history? What stories does this object carry?

PHYSICAL EXPRESSION

184

How do you feel about physical activity? What kind of movement do you love, and what do you dread, and why?

185

What's your relationship with dancing? How do you feel standing on the dance floor while others are watching?

186

Are you sensitive to certain sensory experiences—bright lights, loud noises, particular textures? How do these sensitivities shape your daily choices?

187

Are there any physical activities you've done that you are particularly proud of? Anything you hope to one day accomplish?

188

How do you feel about your body image? Is there anything you would like me to keep in mind to be most supportive of you?

189

What messages did you receive about your body when you were growing up? How has your relationship with your body changed over time?

LEARNING & GROWTH

190

Who taught you something invaluable without realizing they were teaching? What life lesson came disguised as casual advice?

191

What subject that once frustrated you eventually clicked? What was the breakthrough moment when confusion became clarity?

192

What are you actively learning right now? What drew you to this particular area of growth?

193

What genre of books do you most enjoy? When did you first develop this love of reading?

194

What happens for you when you are in a "down" place and you are trying to pick yourself up? What should I know about how you would like me to be most supportive?

195

How has creativity shown up in your life, even if you don't consider yourself "artistic"? Where does your innovation come from, and how do you like to express it?

PERSONAL EVOLUTION

196

What belief from your younger years makes you cringe today? What experiences or knowledge changed that perspective?

197

Who are your three most influential people, living or dead? What specific lessons did each one teach?

198

What quality have you worked hardest to develop in yourself? What motivated this intentional growth, and how do you maintain it?

199

What is something you have struggled with for a long time that may just be a lifelong struggle? How can I be most supportive of that struggle?

200

As someone who will always be here for you, how does it feel to trust me with your stories and your secrets? What would you like me to always keep in mind about protecting your heart?

CHAPTER 2:
AFTER THE CONVERSATION

As you complete this chapter, take a moment to pause and reflect. You've just guided your relationship through a series of conversations that were anything but small talk. These questions were carefully designed not just to spark answers, but to awaken understanding, empathy, and most of all, deepen connection.

You've explored early memories, shared values, family legacies, and the subtle ways you both experience safety, joy, belonging, and love. By talking about the roots of who you are and what brought you together, you've begun laying (or reinforcing) the foundation of your relationship with greater clarity and intention.

But building a foundation isn't a one-time task, it's an ongoing, lifelong process. Just as we each grow and develop as individuals through the challenges we face in life, the relationship itself will inevitably evolve as a result. That's why it's critical for the health of a relationship to consistently revisit and reexamine its foundations.

Some may wonder: what's the point of revisiting old stories and memories if the facts themselves can't change? The simple reality is that as we go through life, our relationship to those moments evolves.

Consider that a younger version of you may have believed you had a perfect childhood—only to revisit it later and realize it wasn't quite what you imagined. Or perhaps someone holds pain and resentment toward a parent or relative, only to later understand that those individuals were human too, carrying their own pain, trauma, or brokenness.

These deeper realizations often reshape how we carry memories—and can even influence how we feel, react, and show up in life. So, when we sit in a safe space with a partner we love and take the time to revisit and explore our past, it becomes an opportunity for both individual healing and intimate bonding.

WHAT HAVE WE LEARNED?

As you reflect on the conversations and responses from this chapter, ask yourselves the questions below. Take a few moments to discuss your answers and journal your response.

1. By looking through our past, what are the recurring themes, values, hopes, or needs that kept show up?

    _____

    _____

    _____

2. How might we give these themes additional attention, so they strengthen and support our relationship identity?

    _____

    _____

    _____

3. What differences did we identify between our backgrounds, experiences, or emotional wiring?

    _____

    _____

    _____

4. How might these differences show up in our relationship?

_____

_____

_____

5. What commitments can we make to each other to help ensure these differences do not divide us?

_____

_____

_____

6. What were some moments from our conversations that felt especially meaningful, and why?

_____

_____

_____

7. What is something I learned about my partner that made me love and appreciate them even more?

_____

_____

_____

8. What is something about you I am curious to learn more about in the future, and why?

    _____

    _____

    _____

9. What are some ways our relationship will be stronger as a result of the conversations we've discussed in this chapter?

    _____

    _____

    _____

CHAPTER 3

Strengthening Our Relationship

"Love is composed of a single soul inhabiting two bodies."

— *ATTRIBUTED TO PLATO*

Strengthening Our Relationship

What happens when two separate "I's" become a "we"? Something remarkable emerges: a partnership with its own rhythms, personality, and strengths that exist nowhere else on earth.

Healthy couples create their own relationship culture: inside jokes, shared rituals, familiar glances, and a unique way of being together. Relationship expert Esther Perel calls this the third entity: it's not just you and not just your partner, but the relationship itself is a living, breathing connection that carries its own needs, moods, and identity.

When a couple nurtures their relationship, they jointly create something incredible together. It doesn't mean that either individual is lost in the shadow of the overall relationship, but, like two architects collaborating on an extraordinary structure, you each bring your own tools and vision. In the end, what you build together is far greater than either of you could have created alone.

This shared identity is profoundly unique and sometimes complicated. The way you balance independence and togetherness, how you navigate stress or celebrate victories, the inside jokes and language you've developed together, or the values you uphold, all adds up to a relationship fingerprint that no one else shares.

Too often, couples allow their relationship to develop on its own, without much intentional guidance. They go about their busy daily lives, and inevitably in the background, without even trying, patterns form and habits begin to take hold.

A couple who might decompress before bed by scrolling endlessly on their phones may not realize that they are also creating a culture of disconnection. Before long, that aspect of the relationship has taken on a life of its own. It can then be difficult to walk it back and make changes when the inevitable challenges start to surface.

Having these conversations can help you verbalize much of what tends to remain unspoken for many couples. The questions in this chapter help you step back and observe this "third entity." You'll explore how you function as a team, what makes your dynamic unique, and how you've grown together through life's inevitable storms. You might notice strengths you've taken for granted or patterns that have never been named...until now.

While you engage in these questions, try to imagine your relationship sitting beside you, much as you would picture a child at the table who requires care, attention and nurturing. As you notice your relationship near you, try to shift your attention from within your own thoughts and feelings, to the delicate needs of the relationship itself. Try to hear what the relationship might be asking of you to help it feel more secure. By engaging in this small shift in your attention, you go from participant to co-creator, feeling a shared sense of ownership and responsibility to ensure the ideal health and wellbeing of your relationship.

SHARED JOY AND PLEASURE

201

What types of shared experiences consistently bring us the most genuine enjoyment together? What makes these moments special? How might we create more of these experiences intentionally?

202

How would you describe our unique sense of humor or playfulness as a couple? What inside jokes or references hold special meaning?

203

When do you feel we're most alive and present together? What situations or activities create that energy?

204

What forms of pleasure do you think we cultivate well in our relationship? Are there areas of delight you'd like to explore more?

205

☐ Can you recall a moment when we laughed uncontrollably together? How does that feeling impact our connection?

206

☐ When life becomes serious or stressful, how do we reclaim lightness and joy? What reliably shifts our energy?

207

☐ What adventures or new experiences would you like us to share? How might these add new dimensions to our enjoyment of life together? What's one experience we could plan soon?

TRUST & SECURITY

208

☐ What helps you feel most secure and trusted in our relationship? How might we strengthen this foundation together?

209

Are there things that trigger or test our foundation of trust? How can we work together as a team to avoid those situations?

210

How do you experience our ability to be vulnerable with each other? What conditions or behaviors make this vulnerability feel safe? How could we create even greater emotional safety for one another?

211

When have you felt most deeply that I had your back no matter what? What about that situation demonstrated trustworthiness? How can we consistently show this kind of support to each other?

212

What promises—spoken or unspoken—do you feel we've made to each other that form the bedrock of our partnership? Are there promises we should revisit or make more explicit?

213

What fears or insecurities do you find easiest to share with me? Which ones feel more challenging to express? What might make it safer to discuss these vulnerable areas together?

214

How do you think we balance transparency with healthy privacy in our relationship? Are there areas where you'd like to adjust this balance? What boundaries around information feel right for us?

215

Are there things we tend to do or say to each other that promote reassurance, trust, and togetherness in our relationship? Can you give any examples?

OUR PARTNERSHIP

216

What does it feel like for you when I have your back? Can you share any examples?

217

When do you feel our partnership is strongest? What elements or circumstances bring out the best in us as a unit?

218

Under what circumstances does it feel like we are "two ships passing in the night" rather than acting as a team? What could we do to avoid that happening?

219

How would you describe the unique culture we've created in our relationship? What values, habits, or unspoken agreements define "us"?

220

If our relationship had a personality distinct from either of us individually, how would you describe it? What qualities would you highlight? How might we nurture the best of these traits?

221

☐ Do you feel we are succeeding at living by our goals and values? How can we do a better job?

222

☐ How has your sense of "we" evolved since we first came together? What events stand out as strengthening us as a team?

223

☐ Are there situations that make it harder for us to work as a team? What are some ways that we can improve our sense of partnership and teamwork?

224

☐ How do you think others perceive us as a unit? Does this public perception differ from how you experience us from the inside?

MUTUAL GROWTH & SUPPORT

225

How could we better encourage each other's personal development while strengthening our shared bond? Can you share specific examples?

226

What strengths do you think we've helped develop in each other that might have remained dormant otherwise? How might we continue to nurture these qualities in one another?

227

How do you experience the balance between independence and togetherness in our relationship? Are there areas where you'd like to adjust this balance?

228

What have you learned about yourself through being with me that might have taken longer to discover otherwise? How can we continue to serve as mirrors for each other's growth?

229

When one of us struggles, does the other get dragged down, or do they step up? How might we support each other more during individual struggles?

230

In what ways do we bring out the best in each other? How might we enhance the positive influences while minimizing the difficult ones?

SHARED RESILIENCE

231

Think about a challenge we navigated successfully— what specific strengths did we draw on that helped us through? How can we intentionally apply these strengths to future challenges?

232

What qualities or actions make us resilient as a team when facing external challenges? How might we strengthen these capacities even further?

233

How do you experience our ability to bounce back from disappointments or setbacks together? What helps us recover as a unit?

234

When life feels overwhelming, what aspects of our relationship provide stability or grounding for you? How might we protect and enhance these stabilizing elements?

235

What patterns have you noticed in how we immediately respond to stressors or problems? How do these responses evolve as we work through issues? Are there adjustments we could make to respond more effectively?

236

When unexpected changes disrupt our plans or routines, how do we typically respond? What helps us remain calm and flexible?

237

What gives you confidence in our ability to handle future challenges that may arise? How have past experiences shaped this trust?

STRIKING BALANCE TOGETHER

238

How do you think our different strengths complement each other? Can you share an example?

239

What differences between us do you find most challenging, and which do you find the most enriching? How can we better appreciate these contrasts?

240

What roles do you notice us naturally falling into when working together? How do these dynamics serve us or sometimes limit us? Would you change anything?

241

When we have a difference of opinions, how does it tend to unfold? Are there things we can do to better accommodate each other's viewpoints?

242

In what ways do you think we balance each other emotionally? How does this impact us as a couple?

243

How do you feel about the division of responsibilities between us? What adjustments might create a more satisfying balance?

Our Values & Vision

244

What core values stand as the foundation for us as a couple? How do these principles guide our decisions or actions?

245

What are some examples of where we strongly align for our future goals?

246

Where do our future goals seem to differ? How might we bridge any gaps in our visions?

247

What aspects of our relationship do you most hope will always burn brightly, regardless of what comes our way? How can we protect and nurture these essential qualities together?

248

What tends to happen to "us" when you and I hold different values or views? What can we do to help us find and maintain mutual respect and common ground?

249

What legacy or impact would you like us to create together, whether in our immediate circle or the broader world? What steps could we take to manifest this shared purpose?

250

How do our shared ethics or principles show up in practical, everyday decisions? Can you share an example?

251

Think about our most recent disagreement about money. What underlying values or concerns were really at play, and how could we better approach similar situations in the future?

252

How do you think we balance honoring traditions with creating new ones that reflect our evolving values? Are there traditions we should reconsider or new rituals we might wish to establish?

OUR DAILY RHYTHMS & RITUALS

253

What routines or rituals have we created that feel uniquely "us"? How do these patterns strengthen our connection?

254

How do we do as a couple with our daily transitions—waking up, reconnecting after time apart, winding down together? How might we enhance these transition points to build more connection?

255

What small gestures or daily habits make you feel particularly loved—even if they are sweet and simple?

256

What rituals help us reconnect after busy periods or time apart? What new reconnection practices might we explore to enhance our reuniting moments?

257

What specific household responsibility creates the most tension between us? How has this affected our relationship, and what concrete steps could we take to improve this dynamic?

258

When we're both overscheduled and exhausted, what tends to break down first in our relationship? What things could we say or do to help bolster our relationship in those moments?

NAVIGATING CHALLENGES TOGETHER

259

How would you describe our conflict style as a couple? What patterns have you noticed in how we handle disagreements?

260

What's one recurring argument we have that feels like a broken record? What can we do to better honor each other's viewpoints without pushing for a resolution?

261

How do our different approaches to technology (phones, social media, screens) impact our daily interactions? Can you describe a specific instance where this created connection or distance?

262

What helps us find our way back to alignment after we've been disconnected or at odds? What repair strategies work best and why?

263

How do external pressures or stressors affect our relationship? What could we do to stay more connected during those times?

264

How do we do when it comes to setting external boundaries with others (work, friends, family)? Are there steps we can take to better protect our relationship?

265

Is there a particular challenge we tend to face that actually makes us stronger rather than drives us apart? Why do you think that happens?

266

What signals or indicators help you recognize when we're approaching a conflict? Do you feel any shifts in your body? What can we say or do to stay connected when we notice the sounding of those alarms?

267

If we ever vent to unload stress from work, how should the listener know whether to offer advice or just create a safe space to listen and validate? Can you give an example?

268

What external stressor (work, family, finances) has been most challenging for our relationship in the past year? How did we handle it, and what could we have done differently?

269

How has our relationship with each of our families affected us as a couple? What specific boundaries or adjustments might improve how we navigate family dynamics?

SHARED INTIMACY

270

What does safety look like in our relationship? How does it make you feel?

271

What are some moments when you feel most accepted by me? Can you give examples?

272

What are some things I do that give you the feeling of emotional intimacy?

273

What barriers or hesitations do you sometimes feel about sharing your complete self with me? What might help dissolve these obstacles?

274

How do you prioritize different dimensions of intimacy, such as emotional, intellectual, physical, sexual, and spiritual? Which ones could we try harder to strengthen?

275

What do we understand about each other that others might not see or appreciate about us individually? How does this deep knowing strengthen our bond?

276

How would you describe the evolution of our emotional intimacy over time? What were some of the more defining moments that stand out in your mind?

OUR COMMUNICATION

277

When do we communicate most effectively as a team? How does it feel when we are in sync?

278

What conversations or activities help you feel most deeply connected to me? What makes these interactions special?

279

How do we do as a couple when it comes to communicating our emotions? What about our needs?

280

Are there ways we communicate with each other that tend to be counterproductive? How can we replace those patterns?

281

Do you think we could do a better job of expressing gratitude and compliments to each other? What are some things you'd enjoy hearing me say more often?

SHARED MEANING & PURPOSE

282

How do you think our relationship has evolved in terms of depth or breadth since we first connected? Where do you see us continuing to develop as partners?

283

When do you feel most aligned with me in terms of purpose or direction? What creates that sense of moving forward together?

284

☐ What do you believe we've built together that neither of us could have created alone? How did our combined strengths make this possible?

285

☐ In what situations do you feel our partnership gives you greater confidence than you might have on your own? How can we continue to embolden each other in meaningful ways?

286

☐ What lessons about relationships do you think we're learning together that might serve us in the future? How can we turn those lessons into action?

THE EBB & FLOW OF OUR RELATIONSHIP

287

☐ How do we each feel when it comes to giving and receiving feedback? How could we make this exchange more comfortable and constructive?

288

□ What's one of your happiest memories of us together? What elements of that experience could we intentionally recreate more often?

289

□ When have you felt most disappointed in how I showed up (or didn't show up) for you? What would have made a meaningful difference in that situation?

290

□ When have you felt most proud of how we handled a challenge together? Are there any areas that we should intentionally strengthen to help us in the future?

291

□ What moment in our relationship made you question whether we would last? What helped restore your confidence in us?

292

What's a situation we tend to face together that you know in advance will be stressful? How does it feel leading it up to it? How can we handle it better together as a team?

293

What do we tend to neglect as a couple when life gets busy? What mutual commitments could we make to prevent that from happening?

294

What conversation do we keep avoiding that, if we had it honestly, might improve our relationship? What fears might we have, and how might we create enough safety to approach it?

PRACTICAL GROWTH AREAS

295

What's one habit or behavior of mine that consistently frustrates you that I might not fully recognize? How does it impact you, and what specific change would make a difference?

296

What's a recurring need you have that you don't feel comfortable constantly bringing up? What makes it difficult to express, and how could I make it safer to share?

297

When have my insecurities or past wounds negatively affected how I show up in our relationship? What could make this go better in the future?

298

What does it feel like when you receive my appreciation? Can you share an example of a time you felt particularly valued and why it resonated?

299

Can you recall a time when our individual insecurities collided to create tension in our relationship? What have we since learned about each other, and how can we continue to be mindful of those individual wounds?

300

What unhelpful relationship pattern did we both bring from our families of origin or past relationships? How does this show up between us, and what new approach could we create together?

CHAPTER 3:
AFTER THE CONVERSATION

This chapter may have taken you into unfamiliar territory—not because the topics were foreign, but because they often go unspoken. You've begun to explore what lives beneath the surface: the emotions you carry, the needs you may not always voice, and the deeper layers of identity that shape how you love, relate, and show up in the world.

By articulating how you handle difficult feelings, where your emotional wiring comes from, and what you need most from your partner, you've laid the groundwork for a deeper emotional connection. These aren't easy discussions, but they're essential ones.

Too often, couples struggle not because they don't love each other, but because they misunderstand one another's inner world. This chapter invited you to share that world—your insecurities, longings, hopes, and the quiet parts of yourself that often stay hidden. That level of sharing is an act of courage, and an act of love.

You've also explored the difference between who you are and who you feel expected to be. In doing so, you've taken a bold step toward authenticity in your relationship. When couples move beyond roles and expectations and begin to share their truth—flaws, contradictions, and all—they make space for genuine intimacy.

Finally, by reflecting on what makes you feel valued, worthy, and emotionally safe, you've helped each other understand how to show up—not just in moments of joy, but especially in moments of pain or vulnerability.

These insights don't just strengthen your bond; they create a foundation for long-term emotional resilience.

WHAT HAVE WE LEARNED?

As you reflect on the conversations and responses from this chapter, ask yourselves the questions below. Take a few moments to discuss your answers and journal your response.

1. What is something we each learned about the other's emotional experiences that we may not have fully appreciated before?

_____

_____

_____

2. What are some of the core needs we each have that may influence how we love, communicate, and connect?

_____

_____

_____

3. Can you identify a moment of our conversations during this chapter that you felt most seen or understood, and why?

_____

_____

_____

4. Were there any difficult realities we uncovered in this chapter, and what are steps we can take to support each other with compassion?

_____

_____

_____

5. What does emotional safety mean to each of us, and how can we build more of it into our relationship?

_____

_____

_____

6. When it comes to our individual sense of self-worth, what are some examples of what we each value, and how can those areas be supported in our relationship?

_____

_____

_____

7. What is one habit we can introduce to stay more emotionally attuned to one another?

_____

_____

_____

8. How can the conversations from this chapter help us feel stronger, safer, and more connected going forward?

_____

_____

_____

Congratulations on Completing Volume 1: Strengthening Your Foundation

Bonus Questions:

☐   What **skills or tools** have you developed from having these conversations that you can now use in our relationship?

☐   What is something you have learned about me from this book that helps you better understand who I am?

☐   How might the conversations we've had from this book change how we interact with each other?

☐   What are other areas of our relationship that you would like to explore together in the future and why?

ADDITIONAL RESOURCES

Brené Brown, Ph.D., LMSW. *The Gifts of Imperfection.* Hazelden Publishing.

Chrisanna Northrup, Pepper Schwartz, Ph.D., & James Witte, Ph.D. *The Normal Bar.* Harmony Books.

Gary Chapman, Ph.D. *The 5 Love Languages: The Secret to Love That Lasts.* Northfield Publishing.

John M. Gottman, Ph.D. *The Seven Principles for Making Marriage Work.* Harmony Books.

John Gottman, Ph.D. & Julie Schwartz Gottman, Ph.D. *Fight Right.* Harmony Books.

> https://www.gottman.com
> https://www.gottmanconnect.com

Sue Johnson, Ed.D. *Hold Me Tight.* Little, Brown Spark.

Esther Perel, M.A., L.M.F.T. Mating in Captivity: Unlocking Erotic Intelligence. HarperCollins.

Emily Nagoski, Ph.D. *Come As You Are.* Simon & Schuster.

Ari Sytner, Ph.D., LCSW. *The Ultimate Relationship Workbook for Couples.* Rockridge Press.

Keep the conversations going with free relationship guides, videos and courses:

www.couples-conversations.com

ACKNOWLEDGMENTS

As a couples therapist, I am deeply moved by the couples I work with on a daily basis. I consider it a sacred honor to sit with them in their raw and vulnerable pain, longings, disappointments, frustrations, hopes, dreams, and most importantly, their victories. I have the greatest respect for those couples who take these critical steps toward strengthening their love and connection.

Therefore, it is with great humility that I thank you and every couple who walks this journey of growth and healing. Whether you are a newly minted couple or a veteran relationship, the simple act of choosing to invest time in your future speaks volumes about what matters to you. Not every couple has the insight to prioritize their connection or the courage to explore it more deeply. By making this choice, you're already taking a significant step toward strengthening the kind of rich, resilient partnership that withstands life's challenges and grows more fulfilling over time.

The quality of your relationship affects virtually every aspect of your life: your health, your happiness, your finances, even your sense of belonging in the world. Therefore, by nurturing this core connection and investing in your relationship, you're creating ripple effects that enhance your overall well-being and even spread positive influence to those around you.

For me, this is a journey, both personally and professionally, that I could not have taken without the loving support of my incredible wife and family— all of whom have made sacrifices to support my passions, nurture my talents, and enable me to make a difference every day in the lives of the couples I see. As this line of work is private and confidential, I don't often get the opportunity to share the fruits of my labor with my family. Yet, every now and then, someone will stop us on the street and introduce themselves to my wife as a client whose marriage I helped save. In my obsessive nature to protect confidentiality, I just smile and say thank you. But in those moments, I can see the gratification in my wife's eyes, as if her support and sacrifice is truly making a difference—one couple at a time. There is no way for me to begin to say thank you, but I dedicate this book series and all my achievements to her.

I am also profoundly grateful to my mentors, supervisors, trainers, and colleagues, all of whom have challenged me to dig deeper, work harder, and push myself in ways I never imagined. Additionally, I am eternally grateful to my coworkers, friends, and professors at Yeshiva University's Wurzweiler School of Social Work, who fundamentally shaped my professional persona as a social worker, researcher, and professor. Perhaps, though, it is my incredible students who truly inspire me most with their own commitment to shining their own light into this darkened world.

Finally, I cannot begin to envision where I would be without the incredible guidance of Drs. John and Julie Gottman and the Gottman Institute, whose research and training have completely shaped my understanding of how to help couples through a sophisticated scientific lens. Their decades of hard work have literally reshaped the landscape of relationships and couples therapy, and I pray that their life's work will continue to illuminate the hearts of couples and therapists around the world.

ABOUT THE AUTHOR

Dr. Ari Sytner is a licensed clinical social worker, researcher, author, and internationally recognized expert in relationships. With more than two decades of experience working with individuals and couples, he is known for his compassionate, accepting, and insightful approach to helping all people heal, grow, and thrive—both individually and relationally.

As a couples therapist, Dr. Sytner specializes in guiding partners through the complexities of communication, trust, intimacy, and repair. Drawing from evidence-based methods—including the Gottman Method of Couples Therapy, EFT (Emotionally Focused Therapy), and Attachment Theory, he brings both clinical precision and human warmth to his work, incorporating a compassionate lens of trauma-informed perspective.

In addition to his clinical practice, Dr. Sytner is a respected educator and mentor, serving on the faculty at Yeshiva University's Wurzweiler Graduate School of Social Work, where he teaches and trains the next generation of social workers. He is also a sought-after speaker, blending science, storytelling, and soulful wisdom to inspire healthier relationships at every stage of life. He is the author of The Kidney Donor's Journey and The Ultimate Relationships Workbook for Couples.

Dr. Sytner is a proud father, husband, rabbi, and kidney donor. This book and the entire Couples Conversations™ series are an extension of his commitment to bringing more love, compassion, connection, and kindness into the world.

To contact Dr. Sytner, schedule a session or speaking engagement, please visit: **www.asytner.com**

COUPLES CONVERSATIONS™ SERIES

Continue building every area of your relationship with these companion volumes:

VOLUME I. *Strengthen Your Foundation:* 300 *Conversations to Build Love & Connection*

VOLUME II. *Enhance Your Communication:300 Conversations to Manage Emotions, Improve Interactions & Resolve Conflict*

VOLUME III. *Reignite the Spark:* 300 *Conversations to Boost Romance, Fun, Sex & Intimacy*

VOLUME IV. *Deepen Your Connection:* 300 *Conversations on Core Values, Parenting, Finances, Faith & More*

VOLUME V. **Thrive Together:** *300 Conversations to Navigate Life's Challenges, Stay Positive & Build Dreams Together*

THE MASTER EDITION: *1,500 Questions to Strengthen Every Area of Your Relationship*

www.ingramcontent.com/pod-product-compliance
Lightning Source LLC
Chambersburg PA
CBHW020003290326
41935CB00007B/287